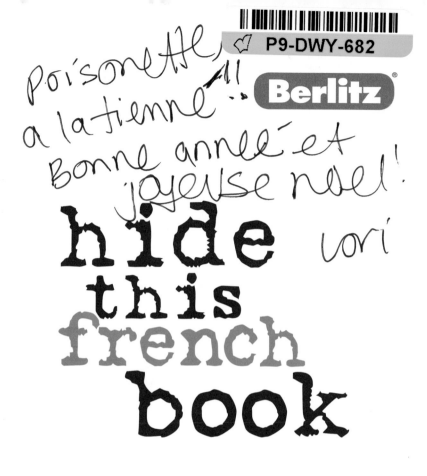

Poisonette,
a la tienne !!
Bonne annee et
joyeuse noel !

Berlitz®

hide
this
french
book

lori

Berlitz Publishing/APA Publications GmbH & Co. Verlag KG
Singapore Branch, Singapore

Hide This French Book

Contacting the Editors
Every effort has been made to provide accurate information in this publication, but changes are inevitable. The publisher cannot be responsible for any resulting loss, inconvenience or injury. We would appreciate it if readers would call our attention to any errors or outdated information by contacting Berlitz Publishing, 193 Morris Ave., Springfield, NJ 07081, USA. Fax: 1-908-206-1103, email: comments@berlitzbooks.com

Seventh Printing: June 2006
Printed in Canada

ISBN 981-246-429-8

Writer: Eve-Alice Roustang-Stoller
Editorial Director: Sheryl Olinsky Borg
Senior Editor: Juergen Lorenz
Editor/Project Manager: Lorraine Sova
Cover/Interior Design: Wee Design Group
Illustrator: Kyle Webster

INSIDE

THE INITIATION

Admittance to French culture requires more than just knowing a handful of expressions. If you really wanna get *in*, you've gotta know slang, street speak, and swear words. *Hide This French Book* has what it takes so you can talk the talk. No grammar lessons, verb conjugations, or any rules here—just the language that's actually spoken in France today—from the most intimate encounters (and, yeah, we're talking sex) to technology know-how (e-mail, IM, text messaging).

stuff you gotta know

It's assumed you already know a little bit of the French language. Most of the expressions provided can be applied to both guys and girls. You'll see ♂ if the word or phrase can be applied to guys alone and ♀ when it's for girls only.

In case you're uncertain about how to pronounce something in the book and don't want to sound like a fool, go on-line: **www.berlitzbooks.com/hidethisbook.htm** and listen up. You may want to lower the volume…

watch out for…

We've labeled the hottest language with a thermometer, so you can easily gauge just how "bad" the expression really is. You'll see:

> These are pretty crude and crass—use with caution (or not).

> Ouch! Be very careful! Totally offensive, completely inappropriate, and downright nasty terms are labeled with this symbol.

We're dealing with real-life French in this book and, therefore, we tell you what the closest English equivalent is—so you know <u>when</u> to use each word, phrase, or expression.

You'll also find these features throughout the book:

 Slang that's really vulgar or shocking

FACT Cool facts that may seem like fiction

 "I can't believe I said that!" embarrassing stories

 Tips on what's hot and what's not

finally

You know that language is constantly changing—what's in today may be out tomorrow. So, if you come across anything in this book that's no longer said, or learn a cool expression that hasn't been included, let us know; we'd love to hear from you. Send us an email: **comments@berlitzbooks.com**. We'll add any hot new expressions to our website—go to **www.berlitzbooks.com/hidethisbook.htm** to check it out.

This book isn't labeled **Un-Censored** for nothing! This isn't the language you wanna use around your boss, relatives, or your new boy- or girlfriend's parents…got it? The stuff that's in here is pretty hot. If you wanna say it in public, that's up to you. But we are not taking the rap (like responsibility and liability) for any mistakes you make—these include, but are not limited to, verbal abuse, fist fights, smackdowns, and/or arrests that may ensue from your usage of the words and expressions in *Hide This French Book*.

BASIC
EXPRESSIONS

*E*verything you need to meet and greet in French.

- ◆ *say hello and good-bye*
- ◆ *ask what's up*

make the first move

Tired of the plain, "Bonjour"? Then relax, smile, and try one of these other ways to say, Hi!

Hello!
Hello!
In French, say it with an accent on the first syllable.

Salut!
Hi!
It's short and sweet.

Salut, ça va?
Hi, how are you?
Drop the "salut" as an alternate greeting.

Hé!
Yo!
A quick way to get someone's attention.

Go ahead, make contact.

– **Hé!** Yo!
– **Salut, ça va?*** Hi, how are you?
– **Ça va.** Fine.

**"Ça va" is short for "Comment ça va?" How is it going?
"Ça va" as a response is short for "Ça va bien", It's going well.*

Pucker up! When greeting each other, the French say "salut" and kiss on both cheeks—in Paris, friends kiss once on each cheek; in some parts of France, they kiss twice on each cheek: left, right, left, right. This goes for women and men. Keep in mind that first encounters don't involve any kissing—simply shake hands. So, get in on the action and say hello with affection.

how you doin'?!

If you want to hang out with the locals, don't forget to ask about their well-being. Here are a handful of cool ways to say, How're ya? *and the right responses.*

– **Quoi de neuf?*** What's up?
– **Pas grand chose.** Not much.

Literally: What's new?

– **Ça boume?*** How's it going?
– **Super!** Great!

Literally: Is it blasting? "Boum" is the sound of a French explosion.

– **Ça cartonne?** Doing well?
– **Carrément!** Totally!

– **Ça va?** How are you?
– **Bien.** Well.

– **Ça gaze?*** Doing well?
– **Comme ci, comme ça.** Sort of. / So so.

Literally: Is it gazing?

– **Ça roule?*** Doing well?
– **Super!** Great!

Literally: Is it rolling?

quick exits

Going so soon? Don't be rude—say good-bye.

Ciao! / Tchao!
Bye!
The Italian "ciao" is so popular, the French have taken it over and provided an alternate, French spelling of the word.

Bye-bye!
Bye-bye!
You'd say it in English!

À plus.
See you later.
This one's short for "à plus tard", see you later.

À tout.
See you soon.
This is a quick, cute way to say "à tout à l'heure", literally, within the hour.

 French hipsters from the suburbs of Paris started **verlan**—a form of French slang—to confuse the uncool. **Verlan** works by rearranging the order of letters or syllables of a word. For example, "ça <u>va</u>" becomes "ça <u>av</u>". Instead of explaining the rules, the best examples of **verlan** have been included throughout this book.

from HOOKING UP to BREAKING UP

*W*hether you're looking to turn on the charm or turn away an unwanted advance, have the expressions you need on the tip of your tongue.

- ◆ *pick up that hot guy or girl*
- ◆ *flatter and flirt with ease*
- ◆ *reject a loser*

pick-up lines

Don't miss an opportunity to approach that guy or girl you're into because French has got you tongue-tied. Practice these fool-proof pick-up lines and you're guaranteed to score.

Voulez-vous vous asseoir?
Would you like to sit down?
This works wonders in a bar or on the subway.

Je vous offre un verre?
Can I buy you a drink?
Look confident when using this line.

T'es trop sexy.
You are really sexy.
The perfect informal come-on to use in a bar or club.

These pick-up lines are cheesy, but they're also great for some laughs. And who knows? They may work for you!

On se connaît?
Do we know each other?
You've probably heard this one about a million times before.

Pardon, savez-vous où est la poste?
Excuse-me, do you know where the post office is?
See a hot guy or girl on the street? Try this line to get his or her undivided attention.

Vous êtes mannequin?
Are you a model?
You'd be surprised how well this one works.

Un-Censored

Tell them they're hot. Here's how:

Tu es...	You're...
adorable.	very cute.
mignon. ♂	cute.
canon.	hot.
un bon coup.	a good lover. (Literally: a good shot)
sexy.	sexy.
à tomber. ♂	hot. (Literally: to fall for)
bonne.	good [in bed]. (Literally: good)
chaude. ♀	good [in bed]. (Literally: hot)

Start a conversation.

– Je t'offre un verre?   Can I buy you a drink?
– OK, pourquoi pas.   Sure, why not.

flat-out refusals

Reject someone like a pro—in French. Be subtle or be bold—take your pick from the expressions below.

Merci, mais j'attends quelqu'un.
Thanks, but I'm expecting someone.
He/She can take a hint.

Va voir ailleurs si j'y suis!
Get the heck out of here! (Literally: Go somewhere else— see if I'm there!)
Get your message across without any hassle.

Casse-toi!
Go away!
Not very nice, but it's crystal clear.

Tu t'es pas regardé!
Take a good look at yourself! (Literally: You haven't seen yourself!)
It's a no-nonsense approach.

Looking for some action? Be prepared for this...

　　– T'es trop sexy. You are really sexy.
　　– Casse-toi! Go away!

breaking up

Fallen out of love? Here are the best ways to break it off.

Ça va pas être possible.
It's not going to work out.

C'est fini entre nous.
It's over between us.

Soyons amis.
Let's just be friends.

Je/J'...	I...
romps avec toi.	am breaking up with you.
ai cassé avec lui.	am breaking up with him.
la jette.	am dumping her.
le largue.	am dumping him.

The "texto" message: a painless and popular way to dump someone. If you're tired of your boyfriend or girlfriend, you can send him or her a "texto" via your cell phone. You don't even have to talk to him or her!

Text Message:	**:---)* Je t'm +. C ni**
French Equivalent:	**Tu es un menteur. Je ne t'aime plus. C'est fini.**
English Translation:	You're a liar. I don't love you anymore. It's over.

*This emoticon—a smiley face with a long nose—means liar.

Un-Censored

Nasty things to call your ex...

T'es* une ordure.
You're a scumbag.

T'es un...	You're a...
minable. ♂	pathetic guy.
pauvre type. ♂	loser.
nul. ♂	loser. (Literally: a zero)
T'es une...	You're a...
pouffiasse. ♀	slut.
salope. ♀	bitch.

*"T'es" is the quick and easy way to say, "tu es", you are.

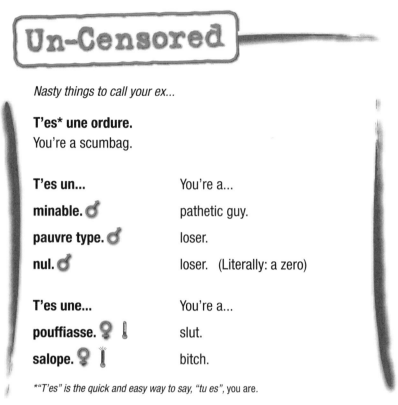

No hard feelings?

– **Ça va pas être possible.**   It's not going to work out.
– **Va te faire foutre! T'es une vraie ordure.**
@#&! you! You're a real scumbag.
or
– **Bon. Soyons amis.**   Fine. Let's just be friends.

 # LOVE and SEX

Arouse your knowledge of the language of passion.

- ◆ *get romantic—from kissing to sex*
- ◆ *top 10 ways to say we did it*
- ◆ *call someone a cabbage—if you're really in love*
- ◆ *talk about pregnancy and STDs*

in the mood for love?

The expressions you need to tell your love story.

First comes attraction...

Ce mec me branche.
I like that guy. (Literally: That guy plugs me in.)

Cette fille, je la kiffe.
I like that girl.

Then romance...

J'ai flirté avec lui.
I made out with him.

Je suis sorti avec elle.
I'm going out with her.

Je lui ai roulé un patin.
I french-kissed him. (Literally: I rolled a skate to him.)

Finally, sex!

On s'est mis à poil.
We got naked. (Literally: We wore only our body hair.)

On a pris notre pied.
We had a good time. (Literally: We took our foot.)
Say it with a wink.

But, for those unlucky in love...

Elle m'a allumé.
She led me on. (Literally: She lit me.)
Though you can use "allumer" for both sexes, it's usually applied to women. "Une allumeuse" is a tease—definitely for her only!

J'ai fait la traversée du désert.
I didn't have sex for a long time. (Literally: I went across the desert.)
Is that dry spell over yet?!

sweet talk

Being called a cabbage or a rabbit is actually quite romantic in French.

Tu es...	You're...
mon amour.	my love.
mon bébé.	my baby.
mon cœur.	my darling. (Literally: my heart)
mon chou.	my dear. (Literally: my cabbage)
mon lapin.	my sweetie. (Literally: my rabbit)
mon trésor.	my treasure.
ma biche.	my doe.

Foreplay, anyone?!

– **Je peux t'embrasser?** Can I kiss you?
– **Bien sûr, mon cœur!** Of course, my darling!

safe sex

Be careful! You'll probably need these:

J'utilise...	I use...
des capotes/préservatifs.	condoms.
la pilule.	the pill.
un diaphragme.	a diaphragm.

Practice your bedside manners.

– Tu prends la pilule? Are you on the pill?
– Non. Mets une capote. No. Put on a condom.

STDs 101

Ask the right questions before things get too hot.

Tu as fait un test HIV?
Have you been tested for HIV?

Tu as...?	Do you have...?
l'hépatite	hepatitis
de l'herpès	herpes
la syphilis	syphilis
le SIDA	AIDS

kinky fun

We've been pretty decent, up until now. So, for those of you who like to party, read on.

N'oublie pas tes...	Don't forget your...
films X / films pornos.	X-rated movies / porno movies.
dessous sexy.	sexy underwear.
menottes.	handcuffs.

Un-Censored

Countless ways to say we did it

Nous...	We...
avons eu des rapports sexuels.	had sexual relations.
	It's the medical point of view.
avons passé la nuit ensemble.	spent the night together.
	An understatement.
avons couché ensemble.	slept together.
	Doubt you got any sleep...
avons fait l'amour.	made love.
	How romantic!
avons baisé / avons niqué. 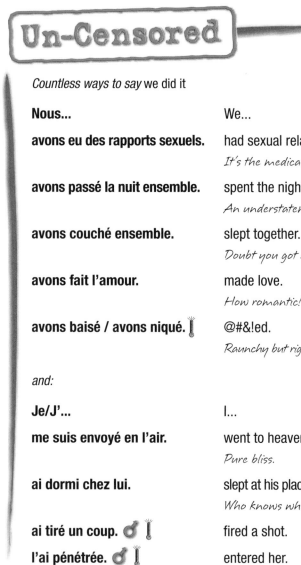	@#&!ed.
	Raunchy but right to the point.

and:

Je/J'...	I...
me suis envoyé en l'air.	went to heaven.
	Pure bliss.
ai dormi chez lui.	slept at his place.
	Who knows what happened...
ai tiré un coup. ♂	fired a shot.
l'ai pénétrée. ♂	entered her.

pregnant?

What to say about someone who's expecting...

Elle est enceinte.
She's pregnant.
The standard way to say it.

Marie est en cloque.
Marie got knocked up.
This one's a bit derogatory.

David a engrossé sa copine.
David knocked up his girlfriend.
Not a good thing, in this case...

Oops!

Brian, an American college student, spent a summer in the south of France with his friend Laurent. To make money, they worked as gardeners at a senior citizens' home. One day, Laurent decided to play a prank on Brian—he asked Brian to get "un seau d'eau misé". A "seau d'eau" is, simply, a bucket of water. But, by adding "misé", Laurent created a very different word: "sodomisé"; literally, *sodomite*. Needless to say, when Brian asked the senior citizens for "un sodomisé", laughter erupted in the home!

GAY and LESBIAN LIFE

*L*ooking for fun in all the alternative places? Look no further.

- ◆ terms for gay guys and lesbians

is he or she gay?

Just like all other cultures, the French have a colorful vocabulary for unconventional lifestyles.

Il est gay / homosexuel.
He's gay.

C'est...
un pédé.
une pédale.
une tante. (Literally: an aunt)
une grande folle. (Literally: a big crazy woman)

He's <u>gay</u>.

Elle est lesbienne / homosexuelle.
She's gay.

C'est une...
gouine.
brouteuse. (Literally: a nibbler)

She's a <u>lesbian</u>.

Warning! All of these terms can be very offensive and downright rude if said in a derogatory way.

And finally:

Fais ton coming out!
Come out of the closet!

Sors du placard!
Get out of the closet!

"Gay Pride" is the name of a gay-rights demonstration that occurs every June in Paris and other large French cities. Gay men and women parade through the city, some wearing colorful costumes. Straight friends and family also demonstrate their support of gay lifestyles. "Gay Pride" has steadily gained in popularity—ever since a gay mayor of Paris participated in the event.

23

5 SPORTS and GAMES

Sports and games—in French? No sweat! From the stadium to the gym, on the field or behind the joystick, don't let anyone make sport of your French.

- ◆ *cheer for your team and insult the opposition*
- ◆ *talk about soccer—because the French love to*
- ◆ *work up a sweat about gym language*
- ◆ *toy around with video-game lingo*
- ◆ *get in on gambling action and the hottest card games*

cheers

Fans, *"les supporters"*, are vital to the team. So, shout out these phrases to motivate the players.

Allez!
Go!

On y va!
Let's go!

Tous ensemble!
All together!

Bouffez-les! / Explosez-les!
Get them! (Literally: Eat them! / Explode them!)

On est les champions!
We're the champions!

compliments

Use these expressions to celebrate your team's spectacular moves and shots.

Bravo, le gardien!
Cheers to the goalkeeper!

Divin, ce drible!
Divine dribble!

Magnifique passe!
Beautiful pass!

Extra, ce but!
Great goal!

Quel match génial!
What a great match!

insults

Don't forget that harassing the referee, "l'arbitre", and humiliating the opponent, "l'adversaire", is part of your job as a spectator.

Vendu, l'arbitre!
The referee took a bribe! (Literally: Paid for!)

Retourne au vestiaire! / Aux chiottes!
Kick him out! (Literally: Go to the locker room! / In the bathroom!)

C'est un hold-up!
They missed their chance! (Literally: It's a hold-up!)

Immanquable!
How could you miss that?! (Literally: Can't be missed!)

Téléphoné!
So predictable! (Literally: Telephoned!)

Va te coucher / rhabiller!
You suck! (Literally: Go to bed / get dressed!)

Quel nul!
He sucks! (Literally: What a zero!)

Il n'a pas fait le voyage pour rien!
What a mistake! (Literally: He didn't travel for nothing!)

Quel enculé / Quel merde, ce joueur!
@#&! this player!

i love soccer

Soccer is by far the most popular sport in France, both to watch and to play.
"Les Bleus", The Blues, are the national team—they're adored by the
French. Get involved in the game!

Mets...	Put on...
un maillot.	a jersey.
un short.	shorts.
des protèges tibia.	shin guards.
des crampons.	soccer cleats [boots].

Fais une passe!
Pass the ball!

Attention au numéro quatre!
Watch player number four!

Dégueulasse!
Foul!

Penalty!
Penalty kick!

But!
Goal!

The "Kop" are fanatical followers of French sports teams—they paint their
faces with the team colors, wave banners during games, and stand up to
cheer their favorite moves or boo the opposition and the referee's bad calls.

But, there's more to life than soccer...

Je fais...	I...
du vélo.	cycle.
du jogging.	jog.
du roller.	rollerblade.
du skate.	skateboard.
du surf.	surf.
de la natation.	swim.

Tu veux jouer au...?	Do you want to play...?
basket	basketball
tennis	tennis
volley	volleyball

extreme sports

You may want to have extreme fun in France.

Je veux faire...	I want to go...
du saut en parachute.	skydiving.
du kayak.	kayaking.
de l'alpinisme.	mountain-climbing.
du rafting.	rafting.
du saut à l'élastique.	bungee jumping.

Are you up for a challenge?

– **Tu veux faire du saut en parachute?** Want to go skydiving?

– **Pas question!** No way!

or

– **J'adorerais ça!** I'd love to!

working out

Get active! Exercise your French fitness vocabulary.

Je peux faire des haltères?
Can I use the weights?

Je peux utiliser...?	Can I use...?
le vélo de salle	the fitness bike
le rameur	the rowing machine
le tapis de course	the treadmill
Tu veux essayer...?	Do you want to try...?
la boxe française	French boxing*
le judo	judo
le karaté	karate
le vélo sur piste	spinning
le tai chi chuan	tai chi
l'aqua gym	water aerobics
le yoga	yoga
Je dois...	I must...
m'échauffer.	warm-up.
m'étirer.	stretch.
ralentir.	slow down.

In French boxing, you use your feet to kick in addition to punching with your hands.

ready to wear

The French are always fashion conscious—even at the gym. Here's the lowdown on the right exercise attire.

Tu as...?	Do you have...?
une brassière	a sports bra
un suspensoir	a jock strap (Literally: a suspender)
un débardeur	a tank top
un tee-shirt	a T-shirt
un sweat-shirt	a sweatshirt
un survêtement / un jogging	sweats
des tennis / des baskets	sneakers

And, don't be caught dead in the wrong workout clothes.

Regarde, il porte...!	Look, he's wearing...!
un bandeau	a headband
des jambières	leg warmers
des chaussettes noires et des tennis	black socks with sneakers

Work-out culture is just starting to gather strength in France and gyms are becoming more and more popular, especially in big cities. In addition to the established, "le Gymnase club", a chain with numerous facilities, there are various other fitness centers. The internationally known Club Med has created its own chain, "le Club Med gym". "Moving" is another chain well implanted throughout France.

pumped up or worn out?

How do you feel after all that exercise?

Feeling good...

J'ai la pêche.
I feel great. (Literally: I have the peach.)

Je suis en forme.
I'm in shape.

Feeling awful...

J'ai un coup de pompe.
I'm feeling tired. (Literally: I've been hit by a pump.)

Je suis naze.
I'm tired.

Je suis crevé / mort.
I'm dead tired.

J'en peux plus.
I can't take it anymore.

J'en ai plein le dos / le cul.
I'm sick of it. (Literally: I have my back / ass full.)

video games

If you're a video game aficionado, you'll feel at ease with French games—much of the terms used in English are also applied in French. They even have English terms to name game tools, equipment, and commands.

Où est...?	Where's the...?
l'ordinateur	computer
le joystick	joystick
la Xbox®	Xbox®
On joue...?	Wanna play...?
aux jeux vidéo	video games
à la gameboy®	Game Boy®
à la gamecube™	GameCube™
à la playstation®	PlayStation®
Tu aimes les jeux...?	Do you like...games?
d'action	action
d'aventure	adventure
de sport	sports

Soccer is so popular that it's played outside *and* inside. "FIFA Soccer" is a hugely popular video game—you're the coach, and must lead your team through matches and championships. You'll need to acquire the right players, figure out the best gaming strategy, and direct your team during the matches. "FIFA Soccer" is updated every year, includes cool commentaries, and comes with a rockin' soundtrack.

play the game

Go ahead—talk to the game!

Vise!
Aim!

Tire!
Hit him!

Tue-le!
Kill him!

Fonce!
Quick!

Saute!
Jump!

Marque!
Score!

Il me reste une vie?
Do I have another man?

Rallume!
Restart!

Game over.
Game over.

gambling

Take a chance.

Tu veux...?	Do you want to...?
parier	bet
miser	bid
risquer le paquet	put all your money down
jouer à pile ou face	flip a coin
Tu as...?	Did you...?
perdu au jeu	gamble it away
tout perdu	lose it all
remporté la mise	win the hand

card games

Try your hand at these playful expressions.

Tu veux jouer...?	Do you want to play...?
aux cartes	cards
au rami	gin
au poker	poker
On se fait...?	Wanna play...?
une belote	belote*
un tarot	tarot *Read about it, on the next page.*

* "La belote" has been the unofficial national game of France for almost a century and is so popular, it's even featured in some French gangster films. It's easy to play; the object of the game is simply to hold on to as many cards as possible.

Take control of the card game...

J'ai la main.
I have the deal. (Literally: I have the hand).

Tu veux couper?
Do you want to cut [the deck]?

Je me couche.
I fold. (Literally: I'm going to sleep.)

it's in the cards

The French have such a fondness for cards that they've incorporated them into daily usage.

Abats tes cartes!
Reveal your intentions! (Literally: Show your cards!)

Joue cartes sur table.
Tell the truth. (Literally: Put your cards on the table.)

Ne brouille pas les cartes!
Don't complicate things! (Literally: Don't mix the cards!)

C'est ta dernière carte.
This is your last chance. (Literally: You played your last card.)

 In France, unless you're in a fortune-teller's salon, "le tarot" refers to an old and widely played card game. French tarot has a unique deck: in addition to the usual deck of 52 cards, it has four "cavaliers", *riders*, between the queens and jacks. It also has 21 trumps, numbered from one ("le petit", *the little*) to 21 ("le 21"). The point of the game is to gain as many points as possible by holding onto royalty—jacks, queens, and kings. Try playing the game yourself—search on-line for one of many French internet tarot clubs.

SHOPPING

*G*et ready to shop till you drop.

- ◆ *shop like a pro*
- ◆ *make a deal and bargain with the best of 'em*

shabby chic or vintage hip?

Whatever your style, locate the coolest boutiques and the famous department stores.

Je cherche...	I'm looking for...
une boutique.	a boutique.
un grand magasin.	a department store.
un magasin de marques dégriffés.	an outlet store.
une boutique d'articles d'occasion.	a second-hand store.
une boutique de fringues vintage.	a vintage shop.
un marché aux puces.	a flea market.
un marché.	a market.

On va faire des courses?
Are we going shopping?

Tu veux faire du lèche-vitrine?
Do you want to go window shopping?

In Paris, it's not only the clothes that are cool—the stores are ultra hip too. You'll find chic boutiques, many with their own design theme (lounge, urban, or even zen) and some with fully-stocked cafés, funky art exhibitions, and DJs spinning the latest tunes. These concept stores carry the newest, soon-to-be coolest, products. Many of the trendsetting items sold in these stores can also be found on the Internet—lucky for you!

shopping savvy

France is famed for its high-quality department stores—they're huge, and filled with tons of great stuff! Use these questions to help you get around and find what you want.

Où se trouve...?	Where's...?
le rayon femme	the women's department
le rayon lingerie	the lingerie department
le rayon homme	the men's department
le rayon enfant	the children's department
la cabine d'essayage	the fitting room
le rayon chaussures	the shoe department
le rayon parfumerie	the perfume / cosmetics department
le rayon bijouterie	the jewelry department
la caisse	the register
le service clientèle	customer service

Où se trouvent...?	Where are...?
les accessoires	the accessories
les toilettes	the restrooms

Need some help? Ask "la vendeux", the sales clerk.

– **Où se trouve la cabine d'essayage?** Where's the fitting room?
– **Là-bas.** Over there.
– **Merci!** Thanks!

Shopping in France may be fun, but who said it was easy? If you're not happy with your purchase, few stores will give you your money back—at best, you'll get a store credit. And your better decide quickly—you only have a few days to make the exchange.

let's talk shop

Grab your wallet along with this essential list of shopper's questions and comments.

Où trouver...?	Where can I find...?
un pantalon pattes d'éléphant	boot-cut pants
un pantalon taille basse	low-rise pants
un polo	a polo shirt
un pantalon moulant	stretchy pants
des jeans	jeans
une mini-jupe	a miniskirt
une veste en cuir	a leather jacket
Je cherche...	I'm looking for...
un sac à dos.	a backpack.
des livres / magazines.	books / magazines.
des CD / DVD.	CDs / DVDs.
des cartes de vœux.	greeting cards.
...sont branché(e)s.	...are in.
Les pantacourts	Capri pants
Les rayures	Stripes
Les tee-shirts très décolletés	Ultra low-cut T-shirts
Les wonderbras	Wonder bras
Les balconnets*	Underwire bras

 In France, the price you see on the tag is the price you pay: taxes are already included. "Les soldes", *sales*, happen only twice a year, after New Year's and in July. It is illegal to have "des soldes" in between these periods. However, you might find "des promotions", discounts on specific items in any store, at various times of the year.

*It's the quick way to say, "soutiens-gorge à balconnets", underwire bras.

is the price right?

Whether you need some sales help or just got to vent about the ridiculous prices, we've got you covered.

C'est en solde?
Is this on sale?

C'est combien?
How much is it?

Ça raque.
It's pricey. (Literally: It pays.)

C'est reuch.
It's expensive.
"Reuch" is verlan for "cher".

C'est trop cher!
It's too expensive!

Vous me faites une remise?
Can you give me a discount?

Vous me faites un prix?
Will you lower the price?

Quel bon plan!
What a good deal! (Literally: What a good map / project!)

Quelle escroquerie!
What a rip-off!

Je regarde.
I'm just browsing.

Je vais réfléchir.
I'll think about it.

Je reviendrai.
I'll come back.

The only places to use your bargaining power are "les marchés aux puces", flea markets, and "les marchés", markets, which are usually outdoors and move from neighborhood to neighborhood.

Confronted by an annoying sales clerk?

– **Bonjour, je peux vous aider?**   Hi, can I help you?
– **Je regarde, merci.**   I'm just browsing, thanks.
– **D'accord.**   OK.

money, money, money

Slang terms for hard cash

Passe-moi...
du blé. (Literally: wheat)
du fric.   Gimme some <u>money</u>.
du pèse.
du pognon.

flat broke

Are you strapped for cash?

Je suis fauché.
I'm broke. (Literally: I'm mowed.)

C'est la dèche.
I have no money.

Je peux te taper une pièce?
Can I borrow some money? (Literally: Can I hit you for some money?)

 Credit cards are rarely used in France. Cash is the most popular method of payment, but the French also use debit cards, "carte bleue", literally, *blue card*. Not to worry—most credit cards are accepted at just about every store.

41

FASHION

*S*lip into this chic chapter and learn how to look and sound totally French.

- ◆ gossip about fashion dos and don'ts
- ◆ name all the clothes in your ultra chic wardrobe
- ◆ pay some lip service to make-up
- ◆ prep for a good hair day
- ◆ enhance your knowledge of body alterations

in vogue

Are you an aspiring trendsetter with a Parisian sensibility? Try these expressions to go with your cool look.

Tu es tellement...!	You're so...!
in	in
branché	trendy (Literally: plugged in)
tendance	trendy
BCBG*	preppy

fashion victim

Don't be a casualty of yesterday's fashions.

Ce style est complètement...	This style is completely...
niais.	cheesy.
clinquant.	gaudy.
ringard / depassé.	out.
tape à l'œil.	tacky. (Literally: hitting your eye)

What do girls wear when going clubbing? The trick is to look sexy, yet not too provocative and to wear something that's comfortable for dancing. You'll find that in France, girls prefer pants to skirts, especially pants with a little stretch in them. A tank top would look nice, but most girls avoid backless tops in order to keep the guys at arm's length. And, of course, many wear high heels—they're the ultimate touch for a sexy figure. Guys, on the other hand, wear the standard club outfit: jeans, cool T-shirt, leather or suede jacket, and casual shoes or dressy sneakers.

* BCBG stands for "Bon Chic Bon Genre", right kind of chic, right kind of genre.

what to wear

Get that "très chic" look.

**une casquette
de baseball**
baseball cap

**une veste
en jean**
denim jacket

**un tee-shirt
moulant**
tight T-shirt

un slip
briefs

un jean
jeans

un pull
sweater

un caleçon
boxers

**une besace / un
sac à bandoulière**
messenger bag

des pompes / des chouzes
shoes

des lunettes de soleil
sunglasses

un deux-pièces
bikini

un balconnet
underwire bra

un sac
purse

un débardeur
halter top

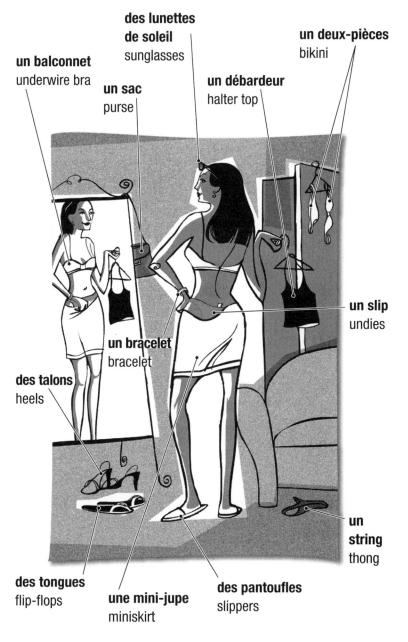

un slip
undies

un bracelet
bracelet

des talons
heels

des tongues
flip-flops

une mini-jupe
miniskirt

des pantoufles
slippers

un string
thong

45

all dolled up

French women have mastered the art of applying make-up to enhance their best features. Here's what you'll need to achieve that chic look.

J'ai besoin de/d'...	I need some...
blush.	blush.
fond de teint.	foundation.
eye liner.	eyeliner.
ombre à paupières.	eye shadow.
gloss / rouge à lèvres.	lipgloss / lipstick.
mascara.	mascara.
poudre.	powder.

in the powder room

Don't forget about those toiletry essentials! Just keep your language fresh and clean.

J'ai besoin de...	I need...
mon bain moussant.	my bubble bath.
mon gel pour la douche.	my shower gel.
mon savon.	my soap.
mon déodorant.	my deodorant.
ma crème.	my lotion.
mes serviettes hygiéniques.	my pads.
mes tampons.	my tampons.
ma trousse de toilette.	my toiletry case.

Solve bathroom issues with ease.

–Tu me passes mon savon? Can you give me my soap?

–Le voilà. Here you are.

46

 You can find great products—and great deals—at any small French department store, such as "Monoprix" or "Prisunic". In addition to medicine and perfume, you can purchase make-up at "une pharmacie", a pharmacy. If you're looking for a lot of personal attention from the salespeople, check out "une parfumerie", a small shop that sells upscale make-up and perfume brands. "Sephora" is a popular "parfumerie" that now has locations worldwide—there may even be one near you!

pamper yourself

Go ahead and indulge in the French spa experience.

Je voudrais...	I'd like...
un nettoyage de peau.	a facial.
une manucure.	a manicure.
une pédicure / beauté des pieds.	a pedicure.
un massage.	a massage.
une épilation du maillot.	a bikini wax.
une épilation des sourcils.	an eyebrow wax.
une épilation des jambes entières.	a full-leg wax.

Je voudrais me faire les ongles des mains et des pieds.
I want a manicure and pedicure.

Most French women don't shave, they wax. Some wax at home; others visit the beauty salon. You'll have to plan your trip "chez l'esthéticienne" ahead of time and make an appointment; walk-ins usually aren't accepted. The esthetician will do everything from your toes to your arms and eyebrows, not to mention "le maillot", bikini, and "les aisselles", underarms. And, you don't need to tip, unless you've received superior service.

hair necessities

For those who just can't afford a bad hair day.

J'ai besoin de/d'...	I need...
une frange.	bangs.
un brushing.	a blow out.
une coupe de cheveux.	a hair cut.
mèches.	highlights.
Tu as...?	Do you have...?
une barrette	a barette
un serre-tête	a headband
des pinces à cheveux	hair clips
un élastique	a hairband
une épingle à cheveux	a hairpin
Elle a les cheveux...	Her hair is...
bouclés.	curly.
raides.	straight.
teints.	dyed.
décolorés.	lightened.
blonds / bruns / roux / noirs.	blond / brown / red / black.
Il a...	He has...
une barbe.	a beard.
une coupe en brosse.	a buzz cut.
un bouc.	a goatee.
une barbe de trois jours.	scruff. (Literally: a beard of three days)
la boule à zéro.	a completely shaved head. (Literally: a zero ball)

body alterations

French fashion is more than just having the right clothes—you've got to have the right body too. For those who don't...

Tu as fait de la chirurgie esthétique?
Did you have plastic surgery?

Je me suis fait refaire...	I had...
les seins.	a boob job.
le nez.	a nose job.
le ventre.	a tummy tuck.

Je me suis fait gonfler les lèvres.
I had my lips enhanced.

Il s'est fait tatouer.
He got a tattoo.

Il a un piercing au...	He has a/an...piercing.
nombril.	belly button
sourcil.	eyebrow
téton.	nipple
nez.	nose

If you decide to get a piercing or tattoo in France, be prepared. Here's how to say—or scream—that it hurts.

Oh lala...	**Aïe!**	**Ouille!**	**Beuh!**	**Berk!**
Oh boy...	Ouch!	Ow!	Ugh!	Yikes!

Tattoos and body piercings are very popular among young people in France. The latest trend is multiple piercings. You'll find trendy French youngsters with pierced earlobes, eyebrows, tongue, and belly button.

49

 BODY

*T*he bare facts—from head to toe.

- ◆ speak up about body parts and body image
- ◆ let loose—talk about burping, farting, and other gross stuff

body beautiful

Here's the skinny on that perfect—or not-so-perfect—French body.

Tu as...	You have...
de jolies jambes.	nice legs.
les fesses fermes.	a tight butt.
de beaux seins.	nice boobs.
un corps parfait.	a perfect body.
Je/J'...	I...
ai du bide.	have a beer gut.
ai des bourrelets.	have stomach rolls.
suis plate.	am flat-chested.
porte des lunettes.	wear glasses.
porte des verres de contact.	wear contacts.

who's your type?

So, what turns you on?

J'aime les hommes...	I like...men.
musclés.	muscular
petit / grands.	short / tall
chauves / poilus.	bald / hairy
aux cheveux longs.	long-haired
barbus.	bearded
avec une barbe de trois jours.	scruffy
J'aime les filles...	I like...girls.
menues.	petite
avec des formes.	curvy
grandes.	tall
aux cheveux courts.	short-haired
avec une grosse poitrine.	big-breasted

lookin' hot—or not

From the good, the bad, to the ugly...

All about her...

C'est un boudin.
She is an ugly woman. (Literally: She is blood sausage.)
It may sound corny, but this is a real insult in French!

Elle est plate comme une limande.
She's flat-chested. (Literally: She's as flat as a flounder.)
Ouch!

Elle a de la culotte de cheval.
She has saddlebags. (Literally: She has horse pants.)

C'est une grande perche.
She is tall and skinny. (Literally: She is a string bean.)
This comment isn't meant to be positive.

Elle est bien roulée.
She has a nice body. (Literally: She's well-curved.)

Il y a du monde au balcon.
She has big boobs. (Literally: The balcony is crowded.)
It's said when a woman's cleavage is visible.

All about him or her...

C'est un beau morceau.
He/She is a handsome morsel.
Absolutely delicious, right?!

Quel canon!
What a knock-out!
It's usually said with the mouth wide open.

All about him...

Quel gros lard! ♂
What a fat slob! (Literally: What a fat piece of bacon!)

Il est maigre comme un clou.
He is skin and bones. (Literally: He is skinny as a nail.)

Some may find this characteristic appealing...

Quel beau gosse.
What a handsome guy. (Literally: What a handsome kid.)

Il est bien foutu.
He has a great body. (Literally: He's well-made.)

Il est baraqué.
He is well-built. (Literally: He is built like a house.)

Il est carrément sexy.
He is so sexy.

Il a de la gueule.
He is striking.

A young American man was living in Paris for a year. He loved doing his shopping in the little stores around his neighborhood—especially the butcher's, since it was run by women. One day he decided to try one of their specialties, blood sausage. But instead of saying, "Vous avez du boudin?", *Do you have blood sausage?* he said, "vous êtes un boudin", *you are an ugly woman*; literally, *you are a blood sausage*—quite an insult in French. He had to find a different butcher from then on!

body parts

┌─────────────────────────────┐
│ ⚡ *Warning! The language on* │
│ *this page can be pretty hot!* │
└─────────────────────────────┘

Body parts don't have to be
private parts!

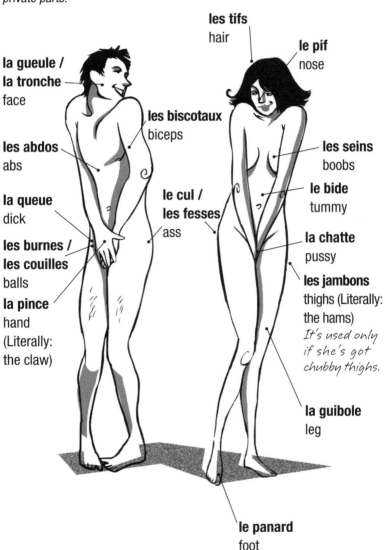

les tifs
hair

le pif
nose

la gueule /
la tronche
face

les biscotaux
biceps

les seins
boobs

les abdos
abs

le bide
tummy

la queue
dick

le cul /
les fesses
ass

la chatte
pussy

les burnes /
les couilles
balls

les jambons
thighs (Literally:
the hams)
It's used only
if she's got
chubby thighs.

la pince
hand
(Literally:
the claw)

la guibole
leg

le panard
foot

body functions

Ew! Disgusting! Here's how they say it in French!

J'ai besoin de...	I have to...
roter.	burp.
chier.	crap.
péter.	fart.
pisser.	piss.
dégueuler.	puke.
gerber.	throw-up.
	Say it in verlan: "béger".

Tu pues la transpiration!
You've got BO! (Literally: You reek of perspiration!)

Tu schlingues!
You stink!

gross

And, totally nasty things that happen to your body...

Quel désastre! J'ai...	What a disaster! I have...
de l'acné.	acne.
des points noirs.	blackheads.
un bouton.	a pimple.
une mauvaise haleine.	bad breath.
une verrue.	a wart.
une éruption de boutons.	a rash.
des crampes.	cramps.
des crampes au ventre.	menstrual cramps.
des pertes.	discharge.
la diarrhée.	diarrhea.
les pieds qui puent.	smelly feet.

 # TECHNOLOGY

*C*ompute French technology talk with ease.

- ◆ process computer lingo and netspeak
- ◆ communicate by e-mail, IM, and in chat rooms
- ◆ fall in love with web personals
- ◆ learn how to phone friends and send text messages

computers, internet, and e-mail

Boot up, save, or escape—it's all here!

Tu as vu...	Check out...
ce super ordinateur / ordi.	this cool computer.
cette super machine.	this cool machine.
ce super clavier.	this cool keyboard.
ce super portable.	this cool laptop.
cette super souris.	this cool mouse.
ce super écran.	this cool screen.

Allume-le.
Turn it on.

Clique ici!
Click here!

Efface!
Delete!

Appuie sur entrée / échapper.
Press return / escape.

N'oublie pas de sauvegarder.
Don't forget to save.

Tu dois sortir / redémarrer.
You need to logout / reboot.

Mon ordi a planté.
My computer crashed.

Éteins-le.
Turn it off.

internet addict

If you're an Internet pro, you shouldn't have any trouble navigating your way through French websites—much of the language used is in English. Just in case, here are some words you may find on "le net", the internet.

Je vais...	I'm going to...
me connecter (à Internet).	go on-line.
surfer (sur le web).	surf (the web).
envoyer un e-mail*.	send an e-mail.
télécharger la pièce jointe.	download the attachment.
Quel est...préféré(e)?	What's your favorite...?
ton navigateur	browser
ton chatroom	chatroom
ta page d'accueil	homepage
ton forum	newsgroup
ta page web	webpage
ton site	website
Tu as...?	Do you have...?
le câble	broadband cable
une connexion	a dial-up (connection)
l'ADSL	DSL
un modem	a modem
Tu peux...?	Can you...?
te connecter / déconnecter	sign on / sign off
IM / dialoguer en direct	IM someone
m'envoyer un e-mail	send me an e-mail
joindre une pièce	attach a document
dérouler le texte	scroll up / down

* *"Courriel" and "mèl" are terms also used for* e-mail.

e-dating

Searching for French love, on-line? Look no further—here are some typical electronic personal ads.

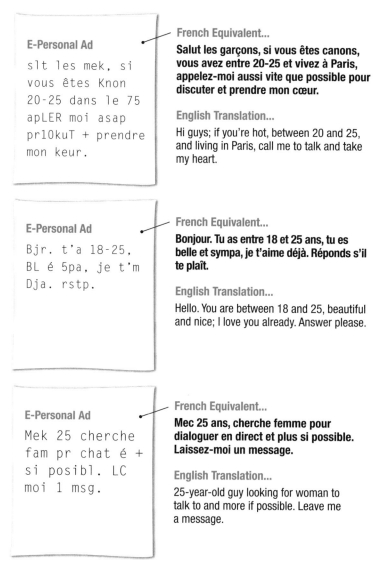

E-Personal Ad

slt les mek, si
vous êtes Knon
20-25 dans le 75
apLER moi asap
pr10kuT + prendre
mon keur.

French Equivalent...

Salut les garçons, si vous êtes canons, vous avez entre 20-25 et vivez à Paris, appelez-moi aussi vite que possible pour discuter et prendre mon cœur.

English Translation...

Hi guys; if you're hot, between 20 and 25, and living in Paris, call me to talk and take my heart.

E-Personal Ad

Bjr. t'a 18-25,
BL é 5pa, je t'm
Dja. rstp.

French Equivalent...

Bonjour. Tu as entre 18 et 25 ans, tu es belle et sympa, je t'aime déjà. Réponds s'il te plaît.

English Translation...

Hello. You are between 18 and 25, beautiful and nice; I love you already. Answer please.

E-Personal Ad

Mek 25 cherche
fam pr chat é +
si posibl. LC
moi 1 msg.

French Equivalent...

Mec 25 ans, cherche femme pour dialoguer en direct et plus si possible. Laissez-moi un message.

English Translation...

25-year-old guy looking for woman to talk to and more if possible. Leave me a message.

internet acronyms

If you want to join a French chat or instant message a French friend, you'd better know some shorthand! It's an essential part of computer culture.

ASV [age, sexe, ville]
A/S/L [age, sex, location]
Start your chat by asking about 'em.

BAN [chasser d'une chat room]
BAN [to ban from a chat room]

MDR [mort de rire]
LOL [laugh out loud] (Literally: dead from laughing)

PSEUDO [pseudonyme]
NICK [nickname]
Most popular French NICKs include: "Captain [name]," "Doctor [name]," "Maverick," "Réplicants".

kékina [Qu'est-ce qu'il y a?]
RUOK [Are you OK?] (Literally: What's the matter?)

dak [D'accord.]
OK

c ça [C'est ça!]
Really! (Literally: That's it!)

l'S tomB [Laisse tomber.]
NP [No problem.] (Literally: Drop it.)

@+ [À plus tard.]
CUL8R [See you later.]

@2m1 [À demain.]
CUT [See you tomorrow.]

A12C4 [À un de ces quatre.]
CU [See you.] (Literally: See you one of these [four] days.)

instant messaging

Reach out and IM someone.

MESSAGERIE INSTANTANÉE - Jean0127 `_ □ X`

Jean0127: slt. koi29?
Marie0817: 1mn. Je V o 6né.
Jean0127: BAP.
Marie0817: j'tapLDkej'pe.

☺

Bloquer	Ajouter un contact	Parler	Info	Envoyer
Block	Add Buddy	Talk	Get info	Send

Instant Message	French Equivalent	English Translation
slt koi29?	**Salut. Quoi de neuf?**	Hi, what's up?
1mn. Je V o 6né.	**Juste une minute. Je vais au ciné.**	I only have a minute. I'm going to the movies.
BAP.	**Bon après-midi.**	Have a good time.
j'tapLDkej'pe.	**Je t'appelle dès que je peux.**	I'll call you as soon as I can.

e-mail

Need that French e-mail screen translated? No problem.

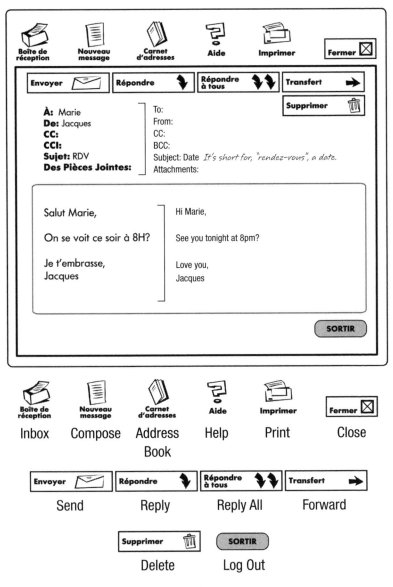

Boîte de réception — Inbox
Nouveau message — Compose
Carnet d'adresses — Address Book
Aide — Help
Imprimer — Print
Fermer ☒ — Close

Envoyer ✉ — Send
Répondre ⬇ — Reply
Répondre à tous ⬇⬇ — Reply All
Transfert ➡ — Forward

Supprimer 🗑 — Delete
SORTIR — Log Out

call me

Want to call someone? Don't freak out! Learn these.

Je peux...?	Can I...?
prendre ton numéro	get your number
t'appeler	call you
passer un coup de fil	make a phone call

What to expect on a French answering machine...
– Vous êtes bien chez Georges. Laissez un message après le bip. This is George. Leave a message after the beep.
– Salut, c'est Sylvie! Appelle-moi! Hi, it's Sylvie! Call me!

phone talk

Dread talking on the phone in a foreign language? Fear no more.

Allô?
Hello?
Say this when you answer the phone.

Oui.
Yes.
If you don't want to say "Allô?" try this.

Salut!
Hey!
If you know who's on the other end, feel free to be very informal.

C'est Michel.
It's Michel.
The standard way to identify yourself on the phone.

C'est moi!
It's me!
Everybody knows you, right?

63

Est-ce que je pourrais parler à Francine?
Could I speak with Francine?
Formal, but to the point.

Je peux laisser un message?
Can I leave a message?
Be polite, for once!

J'y vais.
Gotta go.
In a hurry? End your conversation with this one.

À plus.
Later.
The perfect ending to any conversation.

Je t'embrasse.
Love you. (Literally: I kiss you.)
Use this one with friends and family.

On s'appelle.
Let's talk later.
This can mean: I won't call you.

A friendly phone conversation...

– Allô? Hello?
– Salut. C'est Alain. Hi. It's Alain.
– Salut, Alain! Quoi de neuf? Hey Alain! What's up?

In France, almost everybody has "un portable", a *wireless phone*. Calls can get pricey, so many people send and receive text messages instead of having long phone conversations on their "portable".

text messages

Some short and sweet "les textos", text messages...

je t'M [Je t'aime.]
I love you.

Cpa5p [C'est pas sympa.]
That's not nice.

rstp [Réponds s'il te plaît.]
Answer please.

keske C [Qu'est-ce que c'est?]
What is it?

@2m1 [À demain.]
See you tomorrow.

texto time!

Send a French text message.

Text Message	French Equivalent	English Translation
slt cv?	**Salut, ça va?**	Hi, how are you?
m jvb	**Moi, je vais bien.**	I'm fine.
koi29?	**Quoi de neuf?**	What's up?
RAS	**Rien à signaler.**	Nothing.
tu vi1 2m'1	**Tu viens demain?**	Are you coming tomorrow?
je C pas j'tapL + tard	**Je sais pas. Je t'appelle plus tard.**	I don't know. I'll call you later.

10 GOSSIP

*W*hat to say—good and bad—about friends and family.

- ◆ talk about your friends
- ◆ gossip with your buddies
- ◆ learn to keep secrets
- ◆ talk about your family
- ◆ insult someone's mother

best of friends

Haven't you met the nicest people in France?

Lui c'est mon...	He is my...
ami.	friend.
pote / poteau.	buddy.

C'est ma meilleure amie.	**Elle est adorable!**
She's my best friend.	She's such a sweetheart!

Tu es vraiment sympa.	**C'est un mec super.**
You're really nice.	He's a cool guy.

ex-friends

Is he or she the most annoying person you've ever met? Say it!

Je peux pas le blairer.
I can't stand him.

Je peux pas la piffrer.
I can't stand her.
"Piffrer" is a slang term meaning to smell.

Il...	He...
me tape sur les nerfs.	gets on my nerves.
me fait suer.	pisses me off. (Literally: makes me sweat)
m'emmerde.	annoys the shit out of me.

Don't be afraid to be honest.

– **Tu connais Marc?**   Do you know Marc?
– **Je peux pas le blairer!**   I can't stand him!

67

what a dumb ass

Spreading rumors about the neighborhood fool has never been so much fun.

Il est con comme un manche à balai.

He's as dumb as a doornail. (Literally: He's as stupid as a [broom] stick.)

Quel...	What a/an...
bouffon.	fool.
débile / gogol.	idiot.
tache. ♀	idiot. (Literally: stain)
naze.	loser.
con / blaireau.	jerk.

Je l'ai en horreur!
I hate him!

Je la déteste!
I detest her!

Il me donne envie de vomir!
He makes me want to puke!

Be honest.

— **Quel con, ce mec!** What a jerk he is!
— **Sans dec*!** No kidding!

*"Dec" is short for "déconner", to fool around.

annoying acquaintances

Annoyed with your friends? Be upfront.

J'en ai...	I've had...
assez.	enough.
ma claque.	enough. (Literally: my slap)
ras le bol.	it. (Literally: my bowl full)

Tu es complètement...	You are totally...
ouf.	crazy. *It's verlan for "fou", crazy.*
dérangé.	deranged.
tarré.	disturbed.
destroy.	nuts.
barjo.	wacky.

Tu es si...	You're so...
énervant.	annoying.
arrogant.	arrogant.
orgueilleux.	conceited.
grossier.	rude.

Quel péteux!
What a snot!

Ce mec est chelou.
That guy is shady.
"Chelou" is verlan for "louche", shady.

Cette fille est une salope.
That girl is a bitch.

69

gossip

Have you heard about the latest scandal? Can't believe your ears? Share your shock with your friends!

Je peux pas le croire!
I can't believe it!

Sans blague.
No kidding. (Literally: Without a joke.)

Sans dec!
No kidding!

Tu déconnes?!
Are you kidding me?!

Tu rigoles!
You're joking! (Literally: You're laughing!)

Tu plaisantes!
You're joking!

Oh lala!
Oh boy!

Non!
No!

La vache!
No shit! (Literally: The cow!)

Un-Censored

You've just been insulted? Here are the best ways to react.

Tu me gonfles!
You're getting on my nerves! (Literally: You make me swell!)

T'as pas d'amis.
You have no friends.

T'es relou.
Gimme a break. (Literally: You're heavy.)
"Relou" is verlan for "lourd", heavy.

Écrase!
Shut up! (Literally: Crush it!)

C'est con pour toi!
It sucks to be you! (Literally: It's too bad for you!)

Nimportenawaque!
Whatever!
Don't let this word scare you! It's another way to say "n'importe quoi", what nonsense.

Tu es un loser.
You're a real loser.

Va te faire foutre!
@#&! you!

A little friendly banter...

– **Con!** Jerk!
– **Écrase!** Shut up!

be a good friend

Got a friend who's in a bad way? Offer some words of comfort.

Calmos.
Calm down.
Have your pal take some deep breaths, too.

Cool!
Cool down!
Has your friend totally lost it? Try this.

Cool ma poule. ♀
Cool down, girl. (Literally: Cool down, my hen.)

Relax!
Relax!
Say it when a friend's all worked up about something.

T'inquiète.
Don't worry.

hush-hush

Go ahead, confide in your friends—just make sure your secrets remain untold.

Ne dis rien.
Don't tell.

Tu promets de ne rien dire?
Promise not to tell?

Tu peux garder un secret?
Can you keep a secret?

Garde-le pour toi.
Keep it to yourself.

Tu peux me faire confiance.
You can trust me.

all in the family

Who has a traditional family anymore? In addition to mother, *"mère"; father, "père"; sister, "sœur"; and* brother, *"frère", nowadays, almost everyone has a very complicated family tree.*

Voici...	This is my...
mon demi-frère.	half-brother.
ma demi-sœur.	half-sister.
le fils de mon beau-père. (Literally: the son of my stepfather) **le fils de ma belle-mère.** (Literally: the son of my stepmother)	step-brother.
la fille de mon beau-père. (Literally: the daughter of my stepfather) **la fille de ma belle-mère.** (Literally: the daughter of my stepmother)	step-sister.
mon beau-père.	stepfather.
ma belle-mère.	stepmother.

makin' fun of the folks

*It's easy to gossip about your family in **verlan**...*

Je ne peux pas sentir...	I can't stand my...
ma mifa.	family.
mes remps.	parents.
mon reup.	father.
ma reum.	mother.
mon reuf.	brother.
ma reuss.	sister.

family slang

Just chillin' with your friends and want to use some French slang to talk about your family? Try these:

J'adore...	I love my...
mes vieux.	folks. (Literally: my old)
ma belle-doch.	stepmother.
mon frangin.	brother.
ma frangine.	sister.

Ce gamin est énervant.
This kid is annoying.

Quels merdeux!
What brats!

Tu es une vraie chipie.
You're a real brat.

Poke some fun at your family.

– **Ta belle-doch a des gamins?** Your stepmother has kids?
– **Ouais, trois merdeux!** Yeah, three brats!

the scoop

In France, few colleges have dormitories; the custom is to go to college close to home. As a result, if you live in a big city, you stay at home during the time of your studies. To top it off, you'll end up spending a lot of time with your parents—the typical college career lasts 5–7 years!

Un-Censored

Watch out! Be careful with these expressions; you could make enemies for life if you use them. Insulting someone's mother is a grave offense. If you're really pissed at someone, these very disrespectful expressions always hit below the belt.

Ta mère!
Your mother!

Fils de pute!
Son of a bitch!

Ta mère, la pute!
Your mother, the whore!

Rentre chez ta mère!
Go home to your mother!

Nique ta mère!
@#&! your mother!

Va voir ta mère!
Go and @#&! your mother!

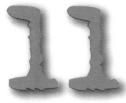 **FOOD**

*F*resh language about food and other delicious goodies.

- ◆ holler about being hungry
- ◆ find your favorite eateries
- ◆ avoid gross French foods
- ◆ talk about eating disorders

you need some food!

Hungry? Chew on this…

J'ai…!	I am…!
faim	hungry
la dalle	starving
les crocs	famished (Literally: the fangs)
soif	thirsty

J'ai envie de…	I want to…
bouffer.	eat.
bâfrer.	eat a lot.
damer.	pig out. (Literally: ram)
m'empiffrer.	stuff myself.

Il mange comme quatre.
He eats like a pig. (Literally: He eats like four.)

Je cale.
I'm full.

J'ai trop bouffé.
I ate too much.

Je meurs de faim / de soif!
I'm dying of hunger / thirst!

Traditional French cuisine has been known for its high fat content. Today, some French are indulging in other types of fatty meals—fast food! Once, the typical afternoon snack was a piece of freshly baked bread with a small bar of chocolate. Now, candy bars and chips are big, and soda consumption has skyrocketed. Fast food joints are totally in.

dining out

Your search for that fantastic little French restaurant has just ended.

On va...	Let's go to...
au self.	a buffet. *It's short for: "self-service".*
au café.	a cafe.
à la cafet.	a cafeteria. *It's the quick way to say, "cafeteria".*
au bistro.	a diner. *You'll find typical French fare here—not burgers and fries, but "steak frites", steak with fries.*
au fast food.	a fast food joint.
à la pizzeria.	a pizzeria.
au resto.	a restaurant. *The quick way to say, "au restaurant".*
au boui-boui.	a little eating place. *It's similar to a dive—a tiny restaurant with less than appealing décor—but usually has pretty decent food.*

Bon ap!
Enjoy your meal!
Use this instead of the standard, "Bon appétit".

Oops!

After a long morning of sightseeing, two young tourists visited a village café for lunch. One tried to order some water, "de l'eau pour deux", *water for two*. But he mispronounced "deux" and said, "de l'eau pour Dieu", *water for God*. The waiter thought he was such a jackass!

happy meals

Time to chow down!

Tu as pris le petit dej / un goûter*?
Did you have breakfast / a snack?

On se fait une bouffe.
Let's have a bite. (Literally: Let's have food.)

C'est...	It's...
délicieux.	delicious.
super bon.	super good.
infect.	foul.
dégueulasse.	gross / disgusting.
infâme.	vile.

Un-Censored

Would you eat these French delicacies?

Tu veux...?	Do you want...?
de la soupe de pissenlits	dandelion soup
des cuisses de grenouille	frog legs
des rognons	kidney
du lapin	rabbit
des escargots	snails
des tripes	tripe
du foie de veau	veal liver

*It's French tradition for kids to break in the afternoon for a light snack.

to your health

There are few vegetarians in France, and health food isn't that trendy, but, just in case, here are a few expressions you may need.

Je ne mange pas de viande.
I don't eat meat.

Je suis végétarien / végétalien.
I'm a vegetarian / vegan.

Le lait me donne envie de vomir.
Milk makes me want to throw up.

Je suis au régime.
I'm on a diet.

eating disorders

Do your friends eat too much—or not enough? Tell them!

Tu es...	You are...
trop maigre.	too skinny.
squelettique.	a skeleton.
anorexique.	anorexic.
boulimique.	bulimic.
gros.	fat.

Mind your p's and q's at the French dinner table. Here's how.

1. It's rude not to finish everything that's on your plate, so don't take more than you can chew!

2. If you're using a knife, keep the fork in your left hand and knife in your right. If you don't need a knife, hold the fork in your right hand.

3. Don't help yourself to a second serving. Wait to be offered one.

4. While you wait, put both your hands on the table, but not your elbows.

5. If you're a guy, make sure the gal sitting next to you always has wine in her glass—a woman never helps herself to wine.

6. When everyone is done eating, don't clear only your plate—pile other people's plates with yours, then take all of them to the kitchen.

 **PARTYING**

Have a bash in French.

- ◆ *go out and have a good time*
- ◆ *fire up your language on smoking*
- ◆ *enjoy a little bubbly talk*
- ◆ *talk about the drug scene*

let's party

Paris and other swinging French cities are packed with cool clubs, cinemas, and concert halls. So go out and have yourself a blast!

On fait quelque chose ce soir.
Let's hang out tonight.

On se fait...	Let's...
une soirée sympa.	have fun tonight.
un ciné / une toile.	go to the movies.
une pièce de théâtre.	go to the theater.
un concert.	go to a concert.

Quel clubeur, celui-là!
He's really club crazy!

On va...	Let's go...
en boîte.	clubbing.
à la soirée de Roland.	to Roland's party.
dans un bar.	to a bar.

Tu danses?
Want to dance?

Je fais une petite soirée.
I'm having a small get-together.

Had a great time? Let everyone know.

Hier soir, on...	Last night we...
a kiffé.	had a good time.
s'est bien amusé / marré.	had fun.
s'est éclaté.	had a lot of fun. (Literally: exploded)
a fait la teuf.	partied. *"Teuf" is verlan for "fête," party.*

up in smoke

Puffing up is still a popular activity in France...

Est-ce que tu fumes?
Do you smoke?

Say it in verlan—use "mefu" instead of "fumes".

On en grille une?
Want to have a smoke? (Literally: Do you want to grate one?)

Tu as...?

une garettci *Verlan for "cigarette".*

une garo

une nuigrav*

Do you have a <u>cigarette</u>?

un clope

un peuclo *It's verlan for "clope".*

For those who know smoking is a nasty habit...

— **Tu fumes?** Do you smoke?
— **Non!** No!

There isn't a minimum age to buy cigarettes in France. You'll find few smoke-free areas—smoking restrictions apply mainly to healthcare facilities, schools, offices, buses, and taxis—and smoking is allowed and accepted almost everywhere. Walk into just about any restaurant or bar in France, and the air is smoke-filled. Law requires restaurants and bars to have a smoking and a non-smoking section, but it's rarely enforced.

*From, "nuit gravement à la santé," very dangerous for your health, the warning label on a pack of cigarettes.

drinks

Would you like a little French bubbly?

Tu veux...?	Do you want...?
un apéro	an aperitif *The short form of "apéritif".*
du pinard	wine (Literally: cheap wine)
un coup de rouge	a glass of red wine (Literally: a shot of red)
un verre	a shot
un gin tonic	a gin and tonic
une vodka orange	a screwdriver
une bière	a beer

Accept an offer...or not.

– Je t'offre une bière? Can I buy you a beer?
– Oui, merci. Yes, thanks.

or

– Non, c'est moi qui conduit. No, I'm the
designated driver.

Going out drinking in France? Beer is always a winner—it's cheap. "Pastis"—anise-flavored alcohol, usually mixed with water—is a must-have. If you're up for something different order: "un panaché", beer with lemonade, or "un monaco", beer with grenadine. "Malibu", the coconut-flavored rum, is totally in. And, you must try candy cocktails—alcoholic drinks accented with French candy: "Shuters Carambar", "Fraise tagada", and "Schtroumpf". These sweet treats are made by dissolving flavored candy in vodka.

FACT

The drinking age in France is 18, but it certainly isn't enforced. You might see teenagers hanging out at cafés and drinking beer, and no one is shocked. Minors can easily purchase alcohol. Perhaps because drinking isn't seen as a big deal, the French don't even have an expression for "binge drinking"!

bottoms up!

What to say before you start drinking...and after.

Ça s'arrose!
Let's celebrate! (Literally: Let's sprinkle!)

Trinquons!
Let's cheer!

À la tienne!
Cheers! (Literally: To yours!)

Tchin, tchin!
Cheers!

Je suis pompette!
I'm tipsy!

J'ai un verre dans le nez.
I've had one drink too many. (Literally: I have one drink in the nose.)

J'ai la gueule de bois.
I'm hung over. (Literally: I have a wooden head.)

Hier soir, je/j'...	Last night I...
me suis sôulé.	got drunk.
me suis bourré la gueule.	got smashed. (Literally: filled my face)
ai pris une cuite.	got wasted. (Literally: took a cooked one)

Make a toast...

– **Ça s'arrose!** Let's celebrate!
– **Ouias! Tchin, tchin!** Yeah! Cheers!

the high life

These expressions are for reference only—these drugs are illegal in France.

Tu fumes...?	Do you smoke...?
du hashich	hashish
du shit	hashish / pot
	"Shit" in verlan is "techi".
du chichon	pot
Je suis...	I am...
déchiré.	high. (Literally: torn)
défoncé.	stoned. (Literally: smashed)
	Verlan: "foncedé".
raide-def.	@#&!ed-up.
	Short for "raide-défoncé", completely stoned.

Je ne me drogue pas.
I don't do drugs.

busted!

Hope you never need to use these expressions!

On m'a...	I was...
attaqué.	attacked.
battu.	beaten.
volé / raquetté.	robbed.

Fais gaffe aux...
flics. *In verlan it's "keufs".* ⎤
poulets. (Literally: chickens) ⎦ Watch out for the <u>cops</u>.

J'ai été arrêté.
I got arrested.

 **ENTERTAINMENT**

*B*ehind-the-scenes language on music, movies, and TV.

- ◆ *chill out and talk about cool tunes*
- ◆ *televise your French boob tube lingo*
- ◆ *get the facts on French films*

music

Get in tune—music, "la zicmu" **(verlan** *for "musique") or "la zic" (short for "zicmu") is a big part of French culture.*

Ce CD est...	That CD is...
parmi les dix meilleurs.	on the top ten.
cool.	cool.
énorme.	amazing. (Literally: enormous)
super.	hot.
tip-top.	the bomb.
Ce groupe...	This group...
c'est chanmé.	is so great. *It's verlan for "méchant", nasty or mean.*
c'est de la balle / bombe.	rocks. (Literally: is of the ball / bomb)
craint.	sucks.
c'est de la merde.	sucks ass.
Tu aimes...?	Do you like...?
la dance	dance music
le hip hop	hip-hop
la house	house (music)
le jazz	jazz
la pop	pop (music)
le rap	rap
le reggae	reggae
le rock	rock and roll
la techno	techno

necessary equipment

What you need to listen to your favorite songs...

Tu as...?	Do you have...?
un lecteur de CD	a CD player
un discman	a discman
un walkman	a walkman
un lecteur MP3	an MP3 player
un iPod™	an iPod™
des écouteurs	earphones
une chaîne	a stereo

 If you happen to be in France on the first day of summer, walking around any city will be music to your ears. Professional musicians as well as amateurs play in city streets during "la fête de la musique", the *Musicfest*, to welcome the official start of summer. You can hang out in a café and listen to one group for the whole evening or enjoy a variety of performances—from rock and techno to classical and folk music.

Rap is as popular in France as it is the world over. Some popular French rap blends American hip-hop style with French lyrics and northern African beats—in fact, many of France's hottest hip-hop artists are African immigrants from the suburbs of Paris. Though French rap music started gaining ground in the 1980s, it's only recently that it's become mainstream.

tune in to tv

Care to watch some French boob tube?

Tu veux mater la télé?
Want to watch TV?
"Mater" in verlan is "téma".

Allume la télé.
Turn on the TV.

Passe-moi la télécommande.
Give me the remote.

Tu as vu le programme télé?
Have you seen the TV listings?

Cette émission est nulle / est cool!
That show sucks / is cool!

Éteins la télé.
Turn off the TV.

Tu aimes...?	Do you like...?
les dessins animés	cartoons
les séries	dramas
les infos	the news
les jeux	game shows
la télé réalité	reality TV
les sit-coms	sitcoms
les émissions / talk-shows	talk shows

FACT Basic TV in France isn't free. In order to receive France's six basic channels, you pay an annual tax, "la redevance". Three of the six standard channels are government owned, and showcase the news, sports, cartoons, and cultural programs—you won't find reality TV here! The other channels offer a more eclectic choice of programming: soccer, recent movies, talk shows. If you're a real couch potato, you can order cable or satellite TV and get hundreds of channels—national and international—at the click of a remote.

french films

Behind-the-scenes movie lingo...

Mes films préférés sont...	My favorite movies are...
les comédies.	comedies.
les policiers.	detective movies.
les drames psychologiques.	dramas.
les films étrangers.	foreign films.
les thrillers.	thrillers.
	You can also say, "les films noirs".
les psycho-thrillers.	psycho-thrillers.

Il y a des bandes annonces?
Are there any previews?

Le film est en version originale sous-titrée?
Does the movie have subtitles?

La séance est à quelle heure?
When does the movie start?

In France, making movies is an art form as well as a profitable business. In fact, with all of Paris's "cinéma d'art et d'essai", art theaters, it's easier to find a great mixture of classics, international films, and blockbuster hits than anywhere else in the world. But don't worry—you can still catch the latest releases in a multiplex on the Champs-Elysées.

GESTURES

We have many gestures in common with the French, for example: hello (the wave), good-bye (moving your hand sideways), it's cold (arms crossed in front of the chest while hands rub opposite arms), it's hot (making a fan movement with the hand), among others. But, here are a few gestures you may not be familiar with...

Ah, sweet success.

"Ouais!"
Yes!

He/She/It is delicious.

"Miam miam!"
Mmm.

You're crazy!

"Complètement cinglé!"
Totally crazy!

chapter 14

You're drunk!

"Complètement bourré!"
Completely drunk!
(Literally: Filled-up!)

Be quiet!

"Ta gueule!"
Shut up.

@#&! you!

This classic French way to say
@#&! you! doesn't need an
accompanying expression!

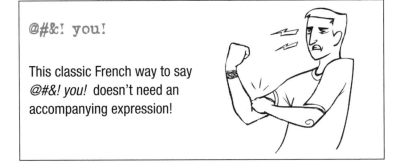